50 Chicken Recipes for Every Day

By: Kelly Johnson

Table of Contents

- Grilled Lemon Herb Chicken
- Spicy Honey Garlic Chicken
- Chicken Alfredo Pasta Bake
- Teriyaki Chicken Skewers
- Chicken Caesar Salad
- Sweet and Sour Chicken
- Chicken and Vegetable Stir-Fry
- BBQ Chicken Tacos
- Chicken Parmesan
- Garlic Butter Chicken Bites
- Baked Crispy Chicken Wings
- Chicken and Rice Casserole
- Chicken Pesto Pasta
- Lemon Garlic Roasted Chicken
- Chicken Tikka Masala
- Sesame Chicken
- Honey Mustard Chicken Thighs
- Chicken Quesadillas
- Baked Chicken Drumsticks
- Chicken Fried Rice
- Grilled Chicken Fajitas
- Chicken Marsala
- One-Pan Chicken and Veggies
- Buffalo Chicken Wraps
- Chicken Schnitzel
- Chicken Piccata
- Cajun Chicken Pasta
- Spaghetti with Chicken Meatballs
- Chicken and Broccoli Stir-Fry
- Chicken Cobb Salad
- Chicken Satay Skewers
- Chicken Enchiladas
- Garlic Parmesan Chicken Wings
- Coconut Curry Chicken
- Spicy Chicken Tenders

- Chicken and Spinach Stuffed Tortillas
- Chicken Ramen Noodle Soup
- Baked Lemon Pepper Chicken
- Chicken Caesar Wraps
- Honey Garlic Chicken Thighs
- Chicken Pot Pie
- Chicken and Mushroom Risotto
- Chicken Cacciatore
- Mediterranean Chicken Wraps
- Chicken Shawarma
- Chicken Lettuce Wraps
- Crispy Chicken Tenders
- Chicken and Corn Chowder
- Roasted Chicken with Root Vegetables
- Chicken Chili

Grilled Lemon Herb Chicken

Ingredients:

- 4 boneless, skinless chicken breasts
- 2 lemons (zested and juiced)
- 3 garlic cloves, minced
- 2 tablespoons olive oil
- 1 tablespoon fresh thyme, chopped
- 1 tablespoon fresh rosemary, chopped
- 1 teaspoon salt
- 1/2 teaspoon black pepper
- 1/2 teaspoon red pepper flakes (optional)

Instructions:

1. In a bowl, mix lemon zest, lemon juice, garlic, olive oil, thyme, rosemary, salt, pepper, and red pepper flakes.
2. Add chicken breasts to the marinade, toss to coat, and refrigerate for 30 minutes to 4 hours.
3. Preheat the grill to medium-high heat.
4. Grill chicken for 6-8 minutes per side until the internal temperature reaches 165°F (75°C).
5. Let the chicken rest before serving.

Spicy Honey Garlic Chicken

Ingredients:

- 4 boneless, skinless chicken breasts
- 1/4 cup honey
- 3 garlic cloves, minced
- 1 tablespoon soy sauce
- 1 tablespoon sriracha sauce (adjust to taste)
- 1 tablespoon olive oil
- Salt and pepper to taste

Instructions:

1. In a bowl, combine honey, garlic, soy sauce, sriracha sauce, olive oil, salt, and pepper.
2. Coat chicken breasts in the sauce and marinate for at least 30 minutes.
3. Preheat the grill or skillet over medium-high heat.
4. Cook chicken for 6-8 minutes per side until the internal temperature reaches 165°F (75°C).
5. Serve with your favorite side dishes, and drizzle extra sauce over the chicken.

Chicken Alfredo Pasta Bake

Ingredients:

- 3 cups cooked rotini or penne pasta
- 2 cups cooked chicken breast, shredded
- 2 cups Alfredo sauce
- 1 cup shredded mozzarella cheese
- 1/2 cup grated Parmesan cheese
- 1 teaspoon Italian seasoning
- Salt and pepper to taste

Instructions:

1. Preheat oven to 375°F (190°C).
2. In a large bowl, combine pasta, shredded chicken, Alfredo sauce, mozzarella, Parmesan, Italian seasoning, salt, and pepper.
3. Pour mixture into a greased 9x13-inch baking dish.
4. Top with extra mozzarella cheese and bake for 20-25 minutes, or until the cheese is golden and bubbly.
5. Let cool for a few minutes before serving.

Teriyaki Chicken Skewers

Ingredients:

- 4 boneless, skinless chicken breasts, cut into bite-sized cubes
- 1/4 cup soy sauce
- 2 tablespoons honey
- 2 tablespoons rice vinegar
- 1 tablespoon sesame oil
- 2 garlic cloves, minced
- 1 tablespoon grated ginger
- Wooden skewers (soaked in water for 30 minutes)

Instructions:

1. In a bowl, mix soy sauce, honey, rice vinegar, sesame oil, garlic, and ginger.
2. Add chicken cubes to the marinade, toss to coat, and refrigerate for at least 1 hour.
3. Preheat the grill to medium heat.
4. Thread the marinated chicken onto the skewers.
5. Grill for 5-7 minutes per side, or until chicken reaches 165°F (75°C).
6. Serve with rice or vegetables.

Chicken Caesar Salad

Ingredients:

- 2 chicken breasts, grilled and sliced
- 4 cups romaine lettuce, chopped
- 1/2 cup Caesar dressing
- 1/4 cup grated Parmesan cheese
- Croutons
- Freshly ground black pepper, to taste

Instructions:

1. Grill chicken breasts and slice them into strips.
2. Toss chopped lettuce with Caesar dressing in a large bowl.
3. Add sliced chicken, Parmesan cheese, croutons, and black pepper.
4. Serve immediately, and enjoy!

Sweet and Sour Chicken

Ingredients:

- 4 boneless, skinless chicken breasts, cut into cubes
- 1 cup flour
- 2 eggs, beaten
- 1 cup vegetable oil (for frying)
- 1/2 cup ketchup
- 1/4 cup apple cider vinegar
- 1/4 cup brown sugar
- 2 tablespoons soy sauce
- 1/2 bell pepper, chopped
- 1/2 onion, chopped
- Pineapple chunks (optional)

Instructions:

1. Coat chicken cubes in flour, then dip in beaten eggs.
2. Heat oil in a pan over medium-high heat and fry chicken until golden brown, about 5-7 minutes.
3. In a bowl, whisk together ketchup, vinegar, brown sugar, and soy sauce.
4. In a separate pan, sauté bell pepper and onion until soft.
5. Add fried chicken to the pan and pour the sauce over. Stir to coat and simmer for 5 minutes.
6. Add pineapple chunks, if desired. Serve with rice.

Chicken and Vegetable Stir-Fry

Ingredients:

- 2 chicken breasts, sliced thinly
- 1 tablespoon soy sauce
- 1 tablespoon hoisin sauce
- 1 tablespoon oyster sauce
- 1 teaspoon sesame oil
- 1 cup broccoli florets
- 1/2 bell pepper, sliced
- 1/2 onion, sliced
- 2 garlic cloves, minced
- 1 tablespoon vegetable oil

Instructions:

1. Heat oil in a pan over medium heat, add chicken, and cook until browned.
2. Add garlic and cook for 1 minute. Add vegetables and cook for another 3-4 minutes until tender.
3. Stir in soy sauce, hoisin sauce, oyster sauce, and sesame oil. Cook for 2-3 minutes.
4. Serve with steamed rice or noodles.

BBQ Chicken Tacos

Ingredients:

- 2 chicken breasts, cooked and shredded
- 1/2 cup BBQ sauce
- 8 small flour tortillas
- 1/4 cup red onion, thinly sliced
- 1/2 cup shredded cheddar cheese
- 1/4 cup cilantro, chopped

Instructions:

1. Toss shredded chicken in BBQ sauce.
2. Warm tortillas in a pan.
3. Place BBQ chicken on each tortilla, then top with red onion, cheese, and cilantro.
4. Serve with lime wedges and enjoy.

Chicken Parmesan

Ingredients:

- 2 chicken breasts, breaded and fried
- 1 cup marinara sauce
- 1 cup shredded mozzarella cheese
- 1/4 cup grated Parmesan cheese
- 1 tablespoon olive oil

Instructions:

1. Preheat the oven to 375°F (190°C).
2. Fry breaded chicken breasts in olive oil until golden brown on both sides.
3. Place fried chicken in a baking dish, top with marinara sauce, mozzarella, and Parmesan.
4. Bake for 20 minutes or until cheese is melted and bubbly.
5. Serve with pasta or a side salad.

Garlic Butter Chicken Bites

Ingredients:

- 2 chicken breasts, cut into bite-sized pieces
- 3 tablespoons butter
- 4 garlic cloves, minced
- 1 tablespoon fresh parsley, chopped
- Salt and pepper to taste

Instructions:

1. Melt butter in a pan over medium heat. Add garlic and sauté until fragrant.
2. Add chicken bites and cook until browned and cooked through.
3. Season with salt, pepper, and parsley. Serve with a side of vegetables or rice.

Baked Crispy Chicken Wings

Ingredients:

- 10 chicken wings
- 1 tablespoon olive oil
- 1/2 teaspoon paprika
- 1/2 teaspoon garlic powder
- Salt and pepper to taste

Instructions:

1. Preheat the oven to 400°F (200°C).
2. Toss chicken wings in olive oil, paprika, garlic powder, salt, and pepper.
3. Arrange wings on a baking sheet in a single layer.
4. Bake for 30-35 minutes, flipping halfway through, until crispy.

Chicken and Rice Casserole

Ingredients:

- 2 chicken breasts, cooked and shredded
- 2 cups cooked rice
- 1 can cream of mushroom soup
- 1/2 cup shredded cheddar cheese
- 1/4 cup chopped onions
- Salt and pepper to taste

Instructions:

1. Preheat the oven to 375°F (190°C).
2. Mix cooked chicken, rice, soup, cheese, onions, salt, and pepper in a bowl.
3. Transfer to a greased casserole dish and bake for 25-30 minutes until bubbly and golden.

Chicken Pesto Pasta

Ingredients:

- 2 chicken breasts, grilled and sliced
- 2 cups cooked pasta
- 1/4 cup pesto sauce
- 1/4 cup Parmesan cheese
- Fresh basil leaves for garnish

Instructions:

1. Toss cooked pasta with pesto sauce.
2. Top with grilled chicken slices, Parmesan cheese, and fresh basil.
3. Serve warm.

Lemon Garlic Roasted Chicken

Ingredients:

- 1 whole chicken
- 2 lemons, halved
- 4 garlic cloves, smashed
- 2 tablespoons olive oil
- 1 teaspoon thyme
- Salt and pepper to taste

Instructions:

1. Preheat the oven to 400°F (200°C).
2. Rub chicken with olive oil, thyme, salt, and pepper.
3. Stuff chicken with lemon halves and garlic cloves.
4. Roast for 1 hour 20 minutes or until internal temperature reaches 165°F (75°C).
5. Let rest before carving.

Chicken Tikka Masala

Ingredients:

- 2 chicken breasts, cubed
- 1/2 cup plain yogurt
- 2 tablespoons tikka masala paste
- 1/2 onion, chopped
- 1 can diced tomatoes
- 1/2 cup heavy cream
- Salt and pepper to taste

Instructions:

1. Marinate chicken in yogurt and tikka masala paste for at least 30 minutes.
2. Sauté onions until soft, add marinated chicken, and cook until browned.
3. Add tomatoes, cream, salt, and pepper. Simmer for 20 minutes.
4. Serve with rice or naan.

Sesame Chicken

Ingredients:

- 2 chicken breasts, cut into bite-sized pieces
- 2 tablespoons sesame oil
- 3 tablespoons soy sauce
- 2 tablespoons honey
- 1 tablespoon sesame seeds
- 1/4 cup green onions, sliced

Instructions:

1. Cook chicken in sesame oil until browned.
2. Add soy sauce and honey, simmer for 5 minutes.
3. Top with sesame seeds and green onions. Serve with rice or vegetables.

Honey Mustard Chicken Thighs

Ingredients:

- 4 chicken thighs
- 2 tablespoons honey
- 2 tablespoons Dijon mustard
- 1 tablespoon olive oil
- Salt and pepper to taste

Instructions:

1. Preheat the oven to 375°F (190°C).
2. Mix honey, mustard, olive oil, salt, and pepper.
3. Coat chicken thighs with the mixture and bake for 25-30 minutes.
4. Serve with roasted vegetables or mashed potatoes.

Chicken Quesadillas

Ingredients:

- 2 chicken breasts, cooked and shredded
- 4 flour tortillas
- 1 cup shredded cheddar cheese
- 1/2 cup salsa
- 1 tablespoon olive oil

Instructions:

1. Heat olive oil in a pan and cook tortillas until golden brown on both sides.
2. Spread shredded chicken, cheese, and salsa on half of each tortilla.
3. Fold tortillas and cook for another 2-3 minutes, until cheese melts.
4. Serve with sour cream or guacamole.

Baked Chicken Drumsticks

Ingredients:

- 10 chicken drumsticks
- 2 tablespoons olive oil
- 1 teaspoon garlic powder
- 1 teaspoon paprika
- Salt and pepper to taste
- 1 teaspoon dried thyme

Instructions:

1. Preheat the oven to 400°F (200°C).
2. Coat chicken drumsticks with olive oil, garlic powder, paprika, thyme, salt, and pepper.
3. Arrange the drumsticks on a baking sheet.
4. Bake for 35-40 minutes, flipping halfway through, until the internal temperature reaches 165°F (75°C).
5. Let rest for a few minutes before serving.

Chicken Fried Rice

Ingredients:

- 2 chicken breasts, diced
- 2 cups cooked rice (preferably day-old rice)
- 1/2 cup peas and carrots
- 2 eggs, scrambled
- 2 tablespoons soy sauce
- 1 tablespoon sesame oil
- 2 green onions, chopped
- 2 garlic cloves, minced

Instructions:

1. Heat sesame oil in a large pan over medium heat. Add diced chicken and cook until browned.
2. Add garlic and cook for 1 minute. Push the chicken to the side and scramble the eggs in the same pan.
3. Add the peas and carrots, followed by cooked rice, soy sauce, and stir-fry until heated through.
4. Top with green onions and serve.

Grilled Chicken Fajitas

Ingredients:

- 2 chicken breasts, sliced into strips
- 1 red bell pepper, sliced
- 1 green bell pepper, sliced
- 1 onion, sliced
- 2 tablespoons olive oil
- 1 tablespoon lime juice
- 1 teaspoon chili powder
- 1 teaspoon cumin
- Salt and pepper to taste
- Flour tortillas

Instructions:

1. In a bowl, mix olive oil, lime juice, chili powder, cumin, salt, and pepper. Toss the chicken and veggies in the mixture.
2. Preheat the grill to medium-high heat. Grill chicken and vegetables for 5-7 minutes until cooked through and slightly charred.
3. Serve with warm tortillas and your favorite toppings.

Chicken Marsala

Ingredients:

- 4 chicken breasts, pounded thin
- 1/2 cup flour
- 2 tablespoons olive oil
- 1 cup mushrooms, sliced
- 1/2 cup Marsala wine
- 1/2 cup chicken broth
- Salt and pepper to taste

Instructions:

1. Dredge chicken in flour, seasoning with salt and pepper.
2. Heat olive oil in a pan over medium-high heat. Brown chicken on both sides, then remove.
3. Add mushrooms and cook until soft, about 3 minutes.
4. Pour in Marsala wine and chicken broth, scraping up any bits from the pan. Return chicken to the pan and simmer for 10 minutes.
5. Serve with pasta or mashed potatoes.

One-Pan Chicken and Veggies

Ingredients:

- 4 chicken breasts
- 1 zucchini, sliced
- 1 bell pepper, chopped
- 1 red onion, chopped
- 2 tablespoons olive oil
- 1 teaspoon garlic powder
- 1 teaspoon dried oregano
- Salt and pepper to taste

Instructions:

1. Preheat the oven to 400°F (200°C).
2. Arrange chicken breasts and vegetables on a baking sheet.
3. Drizzle with olive oil and season with garlic powder, oregano, salt, and pepper.
4. Bake for 25-30 minutes, or until the chicken reaches an internal temperature of 165°F (75°C).
5. Serve immediately.

Buffalo Chicken Wraps

Ingredients:

- 2 chicken breasts, grilled and sliced
- 1/4 cup buffalo sauce
- 4 large flour tortillas
- 1 cup shredded lettuce
- 1/2 cup shredded cheddar cheese
- 1/4 cup ranch dressing

Instructions:

1. Toss grilled chicken slices in buffalo sauce.
2. Lay tortillas flat and spread ranch dressing on each.
3. Add buffalo chicken, lettuce, and cheese.
4. Roll up the tortillas and serve.

Chicken Schnitzel

Ingredients:

- 4 chicken breasts, pounded thin
- 1 cup breadcrumbs
- 1/2 cup flour
- 2 eggs, beaten
- Salt and pepper to taste
- Olive oil for frying

Instructions:

1. Dredge chicken breasts in flour, dip in beaten eggs, then coat with breadcrumbs.
2. Heat olive oil in a pan over medium heat and fry chicken for 3-4 minutes per side, until golden brown and cooked through.
3. Serve with lemon wedges and a side salad.

Chicken Piccata

Ingredients:

- 4 chicken breasts, pounded thin
- 1/2 cup flour
- 2 tablespoons olive oil
- 1/2 cup white wine
- 1/4 cup lemon juice
- 2 tablespoons capers
- 1/4 cup parsley, chopped

Instructions:

1. Dredge chicken breasts in flour and cook in olive oil until golden brown, about 3-4 minutes per side.
2. Remove chicken and add wine, lemon juice, and capers to the pan. Simmer for 2 minutes.
3. Return chicken to the pan and cook for 3-4 more minutes.
4. Top with parsley and serve with pasta or rice.

Cajun Chicken Pasta

Ingredients:

- 2 chicken breasts, sliced
- 1 tablespoon Cajun seasoning
- 1 tablespoon olive oil
- 2 cloves garlic, minced
- 1 cup heavy cream
- 1/2 cup Parmesan cheese
- 2 cups cooked pasta

Instructions:

1. Toss chicken with Cajun seasoning. Heat olive oil in a pan over medium-high heat and cook chicken until browned.
2. Add garlic and cook for 1 minute. Pour in heavy cream and simmer for 3-4 minutes.
3. Stir in Parmesan cheese, then add cooked pasta. Toss to combine and serve.

Spaghetti with Chicken Meatballs

Ingredients:

- 2 chicken breasts, ground
- 1/4 cup breadcrumbs
- 1 egg
- 1/4 cup Parmesan cheese
- 1 jar marinara sauce
- 1 teaspoon garlic powder
- Salt and pepper to taste
- 2 cups cooked spaghetti

Instructions:

1. Preheat the oven to 375°F (190°C). Mix ground chicken, breadcrumbs, egg, Parmesan, garlic powder, salt, and pepper.
2. Form into meatballs and place on a baking sheet. Bake for 20 minutes.
3. Simmer meatballs in marinara sauce for 10 minutes.
4. Serve over spaghetti.

Chicken and Broccoli Stir-Fry

Ingredients:

- 2 chicken breasts, sliced thinly
- 2 cups broccoli florets
- 2 tablespoons soy sauce
- 1 tablespoon sesame oil
- 2 garlic cloves, minced
- 1 tablespoon ginger, grated

Instructions:

1. Heat sesame oil in a pan over medium-high heat. Add chicken and cook until browned.
2. Add garlic and ginger, then broccoli. Stir-fry for 5-7 minutes until broccoli is tender.
3. Stir in soy sauce and cook for 2 more minutes.
4. Serve with rice.

Chicken Cobb Salad

Ingredients:

- 2 grilled chicken breasts, sliced
- 4 cups mixed greens
- 1/4 cup blue cheese, crumbled
- 1/4 cup avocado, sliced
- 2 boiled eggs, chopped
- 1/4 cup bacon, crumbled
- 1/2 cup cherry tomatoes, halved
- 1/4 cup ranch dressing

Instructions:

1. Arrange mixed greens on a platter and top with chicken, blue cheese, avocado, eggs, bacon, and tomatoes.
2. Drizzle with ranch dressing and serve.